WHEN MUM
AND DAD
SPLIT UP

Lesley Ely

Illustrated by Mike Phillips

a di

306.89

To Cally, Jo and Adam

Text copyright 2001 © Lesley Ely
Illustrations copyright 2001 © Mike Phillips
Cover illustration copyright 2001 © Nick Sharratt

Published by Hodder Children's Books 2001

Design and typesetting by Michael Leaman

The rights of Lesley Ely and Mike Phillips to be identified
as the author and illustrator of the work has been
asserted by them in accordance with the Copyright,
Designs and Patents Act 1988.

10 9 8 7 6 5 4 3 2 1

ISBN: 0 340 77899 7

Printed by The Guernsey Press Company Limited.

Hodder Children's Books
a division of Hodder Headline Limited
338 Euston Road
London NW1 3BH

Contents

INTRODUCTION 4

WHAT IS HAPPENING? 5

CONFIDENCE POWER 18

JACK AND EM'S STORY 28

WHO CAN HELP? 48

TALKING THINGS OVER 54

GLOSSARY 60

NOTE FOR PARENTS 61

10–POINT PLAN 62

FINDING OUT MORE 64

ABOUT THE AUTHOR 64

Introduction

You may be reading this because your own mum and dad have split up. Or perhaps you want to help your friend. Maybe you are just interested in people problems.

All our difficulties are easier to cope with when we know what to expect. Understanding makes us powerful – it gives us confidence.

We shall start by looking carefully at what is happening. The grown-up word for this is **investigation**.

Keep an eye out for Henry the mouse throughout the book – you can spot him on several pages.

He is joined by his friends to help explain things.

I hope this book will help you with your problems.

Lesley Ely

You may be reading this book by yourself, or you may be reading it with your mum or dad. There are notes at the back for your parents to read – these start on page 61.

WHAT IS HAPPENING?

It's a sad time when mums and dads split up.

What is splitting up?

The grown-up word for 'splitting up'
is 'separation'.
It means mum and dad live in different places.
They may live by themselves or with someone
else. If mum and dad are **married**
and decide to split up, they will probably get a
divorce. Divorce is when mum and dad stop
being married to each other.

Life has good bits and bad bits.

Some parts are happy.

Happy days are easy.

Some parts are not happy.
That's how life is.

One day we feel safe and happy.
The next day we may feel sad and afraid.

This is true for grown-ups AND children.

The day mum and dad split up is a sad day.

Sad days are difficult, but we just have
to deal with them.
We need **courage** for sad days.

With **courage** we can deal with anything.
We need **courage** for 3 things:

- changes
- losing things
- feeling all alone

When mum and dad split up, these 3 things
give us trouble. They are real **pains**.

When mum and dad split up, the 3 pains give us trouble.

It doesn't matter how they come, **we can deal with them.**

We have more courage than we think.

PAIN NUMBER 1

Changes.

We need our mums and dads more than anything. Being with them is a BIG part of our lives. Mum and dad splitting up is a BIG CHANGE.

When big stuff changes, we feel **scared**.

It's the same for children **AND** grown-ups.

We can't help being scared. It's how our brains work.

We are scared because it never happened before.
We haven't learnt how to deal with it.
We don't know what to do.

When we are scared we get upset easily.

This makes life difficult.

When we are upset we don't think well.

We may lash out at people we love.

We may do silly things.

Even grown-ups cry if they are scared and upset.

This is when our courage comes in handy. It helps us wait until we are used to the changes.

Getting used to big changes takes time.
We just have to hang in there.

Splitting up doesn't change everything.

Just some things!

Perhaps you can still be with mum AND dad.

You just can't be with them both at the same time.

They may not love each other now. But they both love you.

Both of them love you.

Grown-ups' love for each other is one sort of love.
Their love for their children is different.
Mum and Dad's love for their children is special.
IT NEVER GOES AWAY.

Mum and Dad **both** love you
just as they always did.

PAIN NUMBER 2

Losing things.

When our mums and dads split up, we feel lost.
Suddenly the happy times we used to have don't
seem real. It seems like all the happy times
have vanished.

Things change all the time.
But the past stays the same.

The happy times are still there. Nothing can change that!

They are safe in our memory!

I feel like I've lost my mum. She doesn't live with us anymore.

When our mums and dads split up
it feels like we've lost everything.

When mum and dad split up we feel we've lost the way we live.

It's easier to live with happy people.

It's hard to be happy when people you live with are cross.

PAIN NUMBER 3

Feeling all alone.

When mum and dad split up it feels like we are the only ones this happened to.
We feel all alone.
When we feel alone everything seems worse.
The world seems a scary place.

We are not alone!

Feeling sad is okay for a time.

But it can't last for ever!

Courage helps us.
Courage grows from CONFIDENCE POWER!

CONFIDENCE POWER

Confidence power gives us courage for the sad times.

Confidence power means:

- feeling good about ourselves
- expecting the best
- knowing we can deal with problems
- knowing we are loved and valued
- knowing we live in a good world

Confidence power comes little by little.

It comes in 2 ways:

- outside-in
- inside-out

Outside-in...

We get pats!

A hug! A smile! Time with someone we love. Being listened to. Hearing good things about ourselves.

The grown-up word for 'pat' is **'affirmation'**.

There are lots more pats. Can you think of any?

19

Inside-out...

We give ourselves pats. We **pat** ourselves every time we **try** and **succeed!**

Confidence power pats make us feel big inside.

We have courage.

We can deal with anything.

The world is a good place.

We succeed when we expect to succeed. We get used to big changes because we expect to.

Dodge the zaps.

Sometimes our confidence gets zapped!

We have to dodge these zaps.
They don't help us – they make us feel bad.
Our confidence power leaks away.
Our courage vanishes.

Zaps work like this...

Zap! Zap! Zap!
Confidence gone!
Courage gone!

Getting too many zaps makes us zap ourselves.

Like this...

I'm not clever enough.

This seems difficult. I must be stupid.

I'm useless.

I can't do that.

Zaps make us feel tiny inside. The world seems a scary place. Zaps make changes difficult.

We need a 'zap shield'! Zap shields are made of pats. Pats we get and pats we give ourselves!

23

Making a zap shield.

More ways to get pats...

Do anything you enjoy!
Find things to smile about.

Being happy is best.

We feel better if we spend time with happy people.

When I smile other people smile back. That makes me feel much better.

When I make my face smile, it sometimes helps me feel better.

25

Chores help.

Doing everyday things is good – it helps us forget our problems. We can switch them off for a while.

I mustn't forget to feed the cat.

Some people watch TV when they are sad. They watch for ages. It makes them feel much worse!

A bit of TV is good. A lot of TV makes sad people MORE sad.

Don't watch TV. Be active!

We feel better when we are active.

When we are sad it's hard to be active – we don't want to do things.

But WANTING TO is optional. We don't have to WANT TO.
Being active will make us feel better even if we hate every minute.

Feeling sad can make us too tired to play. But once we start to play we stop feeling so tired. We begin to feel better.

Let's talk about Jack and Em.

That's in the next chapter.

JACK AND EM'S STORY

Jack and Em's mum and dad split up.

They felt just as you may be feeling.
They got angry and upset.
They cried and cried.
They thought they would feel bad for ever.

But Jack and Em got used to this change in their lives.

You will get used to it too.

You may feel the same as Jack and Em, or you may have different feelings. You may feel some things the same but not others. Your feelings are yours.

Only you can decide what you will do about those feelings.

Jack and Em find out that their mum and dad are going to split up.

Dad and I have been thinking very hard. When we are together we are both unhappy. So we have decided to make a change. Dad is going to move out- he is going to live in his own place.

It's best for you to stay with mum. You'll go to the same school.

You'll see your friends and Grandma and Grandpa like before.

Just one thing will change. I'll be in my flat and I'll see you at the weekends. It will be different, but we'll get used to it.

Mum and Dad tried to explain.

Jack and Em didn't know what to think.
Nothing like this had happened before.
Jack and Em didn't know what to say.

They felt like they'd fallen off the world.

I don't understand.
It all feels strange.

My head is full of
questions. But I don't
know what to say.

Big change doesn't go in at first.

Jack seems okay about his dad leaving. He's playing like he always does.

He seems okay, but I think he's a bit too quiet.

I don't think anything has gone in. Jack can't think about it yet. He's not ready.

He has to get used to things being different. Right now he can't even get upset.

When big things change we may act as if we haven't noticed.

Change takes time.

At first we may not know how to feel
about change.

Sometimes we feel like we are in a dream.
We expect to wake up and find everything as it
used to be. Changes are always difficult.
Even good changes are hard to deal with.

It takes time for big change to 'sink in'.

We sometimes feel a bit numb.

It's our brain's way of helping us.

It gives us time before we feel bad.

It gives us time to work it all out.

Jack and Em tried to think.

It was very hard.

My home is here but I feel as if it's lost. I've lost my Dad and Mum's upset. I don't know what to do.

Who will get my breakfast?

Everything seems different. Last night I dreamt I couldn't find my way home. The world was different. I didn't know why.

I want my dad!

What Jack and Em said wasn't always what they felt.
Sometimes they didn't say what was inside them.
Their feelings wouldn't come out in the right words.

34

Change confuses us.

When we have big change we feel mixed up.
We feel confused.
Nobody can think clearly.

Change confuses mums and dads too.

Jack and Em felt all mixed up.

Jack and Em went over and over things in their heads.
Everything felt strange.
Before the split, home was with mum and dad.
Where was home now?
They felt lost and very frightened.
Their feelings went up and down.

Jack was very confused.
It made him frightened and angry.

This was a big change for Jack and Em.

It was hard to get used to.
Sometimes they couldn't think at all.
What they thought wasn't always what
they said.

Sometimes they acted like little babies.
They needed lots of hugs and cuddles.

Jack and Em were angry!

Why doesn't Mum stop all this silly stuff? Why doesn't she just make Dad stay? I know she could if she wanted to.

You two are so stupid! I hate you both! No, I won't be good! You aren't good to me- I won't be good for you!

You feel angry. It is hard for you to deal with all this. We are sorry it had to happen.

We are upset too. We just have to deal with it. Shouting doesn't help. We have to work together.

Explosions of confusion.

When we are confused, our feelings go up and down.
We feel frightened and angry.
It's hard to know which feeling is which.

We feel like we are carrying a huge load of worries.
One more upsetting thing happens, and all the worries come crashing down!
We don't know how it happens – it takes us by surprise.

This could happen to mum and dad as well.
They may feel frightened and angry too.
People who feel confused and upset sometimes shout, or stomp about, or cry.
Even grown-ups do it.

Mum and Dad forget that Jack and Em are not grown-ups.

Mums and dads sometimes forget that children are not grown-ups. They expect their children to help them like a grown-up would. If they weren't so upset they would see that this is impossible.

If they do forget, it helps if you remind them.

Mum should talk to Auntie Sue or a counsellor. Jack and Em haven't a clue. Grown-ups have to act like grown-ups. Jack and Em are children.

Jack and Em feel scared when Mum and Dad talk about grown-up stuff. They think they ought to help, but they can't.

Why don't you ask Auntie Sue? I'm too young to know about grown-up stuff.

I'm sorry, Em. You're so clever I forget you're only 8 years old.

Mums and dads sometimes forget that children are not grown-ups.

Mum and Dad don't know that they are making Jack and Em feel bad.

Jack and Em tell their mum and dad how bad they feel.

Tell Mum I'll be late picking you up on Friday. I have to work overtime.

Dad will be late on Friday. He has to work.

Your Dad is always late. He can never be on time for anything.

I feel like piggy-in-the-middle. It makes my tummy ache.

43

When Dad got a girlfriend.

When Dad got a girlfriend I knew he wasn't ever going back to Mum. That was when I knew our family had changed for good.

This is Jenny. She's coming to the park with us. Then we'll go back for tea.

Hello Emily, hello Jack. I've heard all about you. It's nice to meet you at last.

45

Talking things over with Grandma.

I'm glad your mum is making new friends. She seems happy. Remember how grumpy you were when your pal Susie was on holiday? It's just the same for grown-ups - they need to have friends too.

Grandma is right. Mum needs to have some fun, and it's better for us if Mum is happy. Which story shall we read tonight, Grandma?

I'd rather watch a video!

However we feel about things, life goes on.
We do different things, make different friends.
Nobody stays sad for ever.

WHO CAN HELP?

Jack and Em wanted to help, but they couldn't.

Sometimes Mum and Dad got upset. They shouted, and sometimes they even cried.

Jack and Em's mum and dad were the grown-ups. They had to find a way to sort things out. That was their job.

Jack and Em were children. Sorting mums and dads out isn't a job for children.

Mediators and Counsellors.

If mum and dad are too upset to talk to each other politely, they can go to a **mediator** or a **counsellor**. He or she will help them talk without getting upset.

Children want to help, but this is not their job.

Children don't cause split-ups, and they can't fix them.

Solicitors and judges.

Mum and dad decide they will each have a **solicitor**.

A **solicitor's** job is to make sure that everything is fair.

A **solicitor** knows the **law**.

The **law** is the rules we must all keep. These rules are very strict.

There are special rules for **divorce**.

Each solicitor speaks for his own **client**.
Mum's solicitor speaks for Mum.
Dad's solicitor speaks for Dad.
They do everything by the rules.

They may go to **court**.
A **court** is the place where things are decided.
A **judge** decides.

The judge might ask a **Court Welfare Officer** to talk to the children.

Court Welfare Officer.

Making sure the changes are okay for the children.

Hello Jack, hello Emily. I'm Mary Brown. I'm a Court Welfare Officer. It's my job to tell the judge all about you, to help him decide what is best. May I talk with you for a little while?

Yes, we don't mind talking to you. We'll talk to anyone who listens to what we say.

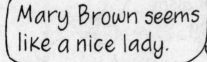

Mary Brown seems like a nice lady.

She has a kind smile. I think I like her.

Things the judge may decide.

Who will the children live with?

The grown-up word for this is **residence**.

When will the children see the person they don't live with?

The grown-up word for this is **contact**.

The judge might also decide about money to pay for things the children need.

The grown-up word for this is **maintenance**.

Mum and Dad worked hard to sort things out quickly.

Jack and Em soon knew where they were going to live.
They knew who would look after them and when.

LUCKY for Jack and Em they get lots of hugs.

Lucky they have Grandma. She's a very huggy person.

It's good Mum and Dad sorted things out quickly. If the sorting out takes too long, everyone hurts more.

TALKING THINGS OVER

Talking is good for you.
Talking gets your worries out where you can
see them and deal with them.
Talk to your friend, your teacher, your
grandma, as well as your mum and dad.

Dealing with a big change makes you tired.
You often need to sleep more.
Dreaming helps – it sorts your thoughts out.

What is most difficult?

I feel okay until something goes wrong. Then I just want my Mum. I want my Mum when I get sums wrong.

Mum and Dad both worry about money now there is more to pay for. Having less money is hard for us all.

I'm okay until Dad comes to get me on Saturday. I want to see him, but I feel bad about leaving Mum. I always feel it's my fault if she's unhappy.

Who helped most?

My Grandma helped me. She's kind and huggy and a good listener.

My teacher helped. He was kind when I forgot stuff. He said I had a lot to think of.

Mum's counsellor helped. She talked with Mum and Mum was happier. That made me feel better.

My best friend helped me. She listened and listened.

Talking always helps.

Helping a friend with a sad time helps us.

It took a long time, but now we are all used to the big change.

We are used to the changes now. Life is different but we are all okay!

GLOSSARY

Affirmation
An affirmation is something someone says or does that makes you feel good about yourself. You can also give YOURSELF affirmations! In this book we call them 'pats'.

Contact
This means contact with the mum or dad you DON'T live with – either visits, telephone calls or letters.

Court Welfare Officer
A court welfare officer's job is to find out about the children to help the judge decide what's best.

Divorce
Divorce is the ending of a marriage according to the law.

Judge
A judge's job is to decide things according to the law.

Law
The law is the set of rules we must all keep.

Maintenance
Maintenance is money for things you need.

Mediator
A mediator's job is to help Mum and Dad find a way to agree about important things.

Residence
Residence is who you are to live with.

Solicitor
A solicitor's job is to know the law and help his client get the best deal the law allows. If Mum and Dad cannot agree, their solicitors can take the disagreement to court for a judge to decide.

NOTE FOR PARENTS

This book aims to inform 7 to 9 year olds about divorce and splitting up. It aims to help them explore, understand and deal with their feelings.

When parents separate, children are distressed. But it is comforting to know other children experience the same feelings. It is comforting to know those children are coping. Reading about them can help.

Most children are resilient. They don't 'get over' the change brought about by divorce. They do learn to live with it.

Confident parents who pick up the pieces and get on with life convey optimism. Divorce is a setback – it isn't the end of the world.

Nothing will take away the pain of such a big change in a child's life. But understanding the feelings that go with the change can make them less overwhelming. Limiting the damage isn't easy, but it can be done.

LIMITING THE DAMAGE

A 10–point plan for parents

1 Explain that Mum and Dad are responsible.
Children often imagine they may have caused
the divorce. Tell them clearly that it isn't their
fault and they can't fix it.

2 Be optimistic.
Expecting a good outcome makes it more likely.
Demonstrate in your own behaviour the grown-up
way to deal with difficulties.

**3 Do everything you can to increase your
child's self-esteem.**
A confident child with a good self-image
will cope better.

4 Keep your ex-partner in your child's life.

5 Keep other changes to a minimum.
Keep the rest of your child's life as routine
as possible.

6 Tell your child as soon as the separation is decided.

**7 Make your child your priority.
Be there and listen, listen, listen.**

8 Be polite to your ex-partner.
Parental conflict (especially about contact) is painful to children.

9 Talk to a counsellor, priest or rabbi, relatives, trusted friends.
Don't make your child your confidante, however grown-up they are.

**10 Make divorce an OPPORTUNITY.
Make your life BETTER.**

FINDING OUT MORE

There are many other books for children about mums and dads splitting up. Ask at the library or a bookshop.

If you are very worried, call **Childline** free on 0800 1111

Childline also has factsheets about 'step families' and other subjects that might be helpful. You can get these from the Childline website:
www.childline.org.uk

Or write to: Freepost 1111, London N1 0BR
(no postage stamp needed)

ABOUT THE AUTHOR

Lesley Ely is a former primary headteacher with a special interest in Personal and Social Education. Her experience includes working with children and parents affected by some of the traumas of childhood (divorce, bullying etc). Lesley believes that learning to talk, think about and understand feelings will help all children. The ideas in this book arise from 30 years of her conversations with children...who always knew much more than they thought they did.